SHOELACE hug

WRITTEN BY
ALEJANDRA VEGA-RIVERA

ILLUSTRATED BY
MARÍA TUTI

Halo
PUBLISHING
INTERNATIONAL

To my mom, Raquel.

ISBN: 978-1-63765-181-0
LCCN: 2022901864

Halo Publishing International, LLC
www.halopublishing.com

Printed and bound in the United States of America

"Shoelace Hug" is part of a series of books for tweens, focusing on mental health. The intention is not to replace the diagnosis of a professional, but to share, through the experience of fictional characters and events, glimpses of what it means to suffer from a disorder: openly, but, above all, without stigma.

This book tells the story of Rebecca: a girl about to turn ten years old. Reb has been in figure skating since she was a four-year-old. She longs to be accepted by her classmates, skating peers, and the grown-ups around her. She is a perfect student who seeks to shine in everything she does.

Reb is about to celebrate her 10th birthday, but the internal ghosts she has faced in recent months prevent her from doing so. Her father works long hours to support his family, so he doesn't realize his daughter has started to develop an eating disorder. However, after several clues, Lisa, Rebecca's mother, realizes that something is wrong with her daughter, and suspects Reb may be dealing with *Anorexia Nervosa*. The tension grows when the family threatens Rebecca with canceling her skating practice if she doesn't start eating more. With love, patience, empathy, and professional help, the family understands that it is not enough to say, "finish everything on your plate."

This text was written with the guidance of the licensed therapist Alma Andrea Orozco Fierro, a psychologist from the National Autonomous University of Mexico, with training in the area of educational psychology.

If you or someone close to you are currently in a dark place from which there seems to be no way out, it must be said now: that's not the case. Although trite, the phrase is accurate: there is always light at the end of the tunnel. And if we are already in the tunnel, only light awaits us.

Alejandra Vega-Rivera, author

4

When I was four years old, I received a gift that changed my life: a pair of blue roller skates with electric pink laces. I learned to ride them before I could even read or write. I skated all over the house, the yard, and across the block.

Two months after that Christmas, in which I received my roller skates, and after noticing all the effort that I put into my new favorite activity, my parents decided to take me to a skating rink to see if I'd like it, too.

They were wrong; I didn't like it: I loved it!

And that's how it all began.

After that first encounter with ice skating, I no longer wanted to go to school. Instead, I could live in that icy haven: the skating rink. As expected, my parents thought I was crazy. Still, I convinced them to enroll me in ice figure skating classes.

My heart skipped a beat. So much emotion rushed from my feet to my head — yes, four-year-olds can experience sensations this intense! The condition for entering skating classes was that I did not lower my grades in school. I promised not to. I vowed to be Queen Elizabeth if they wanted me to.

I kept my promise. I was striving to get good grades in school while attending skating classes twice a week. Soon that wasn't enough. I wanted to live forever sliding on the cold vapor track.

The teacher noticed my enthusiasm and advised my parents to take me to a professional trainer. After some discussion between them and many tantrums on my end, they agreed to give it a try. By then, I was seven years old.

I started training for local competitions. I was thrilled. There was only one thing that clouded my world: the other skaters *looked* different; they were *much* thinner than me. My mom said they looked gorgeous, spinning through the air in their multi-colored outfits, like rainbows in ecstasy. I never dared to ask her if she thought the same of me. I simply assumed that she didn't because my suit did not have many colors, and I could not jump to such height with such fluidity.

The next day at school, I asked my classmates if they had ever, "been on a diet." To my surprise, they had.

We googled many popular diets on my friend Sofía's smartphone. Her mom had given her a cellphone to use only for "emergencies." Well, this was an emergency!

We quickly found hundreds of articles that offered tips to "bring your sexy back" and to "lose up to 25 pounds in a month." I wrote down what seemed most relevant and, above all, within my reach. It would be difficult for me to get laxatives or diet pills. So, I wrote down: drink lots of coffee and detox teas, work out, reduce your calorie intake…

What exactly is a "calorie"? I asked my friends.

"It's like a number for food," Gloria replied. "The higher the number, the worse it gets. For example, my mom says, 'Don't eat that chocolate because it's got 300 calories; better eat this bar of 120.'"

Oh. But how can I know that number? I reacted, intrigued.

You don't necessarily have to know. The easiest way is to simply eat as little as you can," Gloria affirmed with a self-satisfied face. After all, she was smarter than the rest of us.

"You are right; it makes sense."

From that afternoon on, I decided to eat only half of what my mother served on the plate. I also started looking up exercise routines on YouTube from the tablet on which I was doing my homework. I wouldn't eat lunch during my break. Instead, I would run until my hunger went away and it was time to go back to the classroom. Once in class, I had difficulty concentrating, so I put in double the effort.

Within a few weeks, I noticed that my clothes were loose. I felt great pride in my "extraordinary willpower," as Gloria used to say that her mother called *that feeling*.

I managed to jump higher and do several tricks in my skating practices. Excited and with eyes full of pride, my mother said it was time to buy me a new suit! One that would match my electric pink shoelaces since they were my favorite laces. I would transfer them from skates to skates as needed.

My classmates congratulated me on how well I *looked* and also for everything I had achieved in my practices. That motivated me like nothing else had since I was given my first pair of roller skates at four.

My life was pink, like my shoelaces, and I was willing to continue dreaming until reaching *even more happiness*.

Without realizing it, three years passed by, and my 10th birthday arrived. At that point, I had already started to compete semi-professionally in many championships. I would often end up within the first three places. And, well, what can I say about my outfits: I had dozens of them! Some simpler than others, some with sequins, and they all looked *terrific* with my slim figure. But of course, I thought I still needed to lose a few pounds.

The day before my birthday, I won first place in a competition, but I didn't feel good about it. I didn't feel good about myself. I was grumpy and didn't want to get out of bed at all. My mom had organized a party that I didn't want to attend. After all, the guests weren't really my friends; I couldn't afford to have friends between school and my rigorous skating practices.

To encourage me to get out of bed, I'd put particular emphasis on what had become the first thing I did as soon as I woke up in the morning: touch my belly to make sure it was flat. That made me feel good somehow.

My mom came to get me out of bed because it was getting late, but I was exhausted even though I had slept for over 12 hours.

"My love, hurry up. You gotta have breakfast and get ready before the guests arrive," my mom said.

"I'm not going to have breakfast," I replied.

"Why not?"

"I'll eat later at the party. There will be food, right? People believe they can't have fun without food. Also, remember that I have to lose ten pounds before my next competition!"

"What do you mean you *have* to lose ten pounds before your next competition? Who told you that, your coach? She's crazy! You are a bone!"

Mom came over and hugged me tightly.

"Holding you is like hugging a shoelace."

"A shoelace hug?!" I replied, annoyed as I was intrigued.

"Yes, you are as narrow as your favorite pink shoelaces!"

I pushed Mom away from my body with a gesture of discomfort.

"Well, you don't have to be rude to me, Rebecca."

I felt rage as intense as if I had been pinched very hard or hit with the spring of a rubber band.

"Let's see, let me look at you," Mom said.

My mom grabbed me and looked at me from head to toe, inspecting every inch of my body like she was looking for fleas.

"Why do you have so many tiny hairs? You didn't have them before. It's too early for you to be experiencing puberty. Also, you're looking quite pale lately. You train a lot and eat little. You have to eat better."

"Mom! Please leave me alone!"

"Rebeca! You don't get to raise your voice to me. Hurry up, it's getting late!" Mom said, then slammed the door as she left the room.

I began to take the clothes out of my closet and put them on my bed while I remembered what my life was like when I *ate better*.

My classmates avoided teaming up with me in PE. They thought I would make them lose because I was "chubby." That's even though I skated every evening. My aunts told my mother that I was pretty and that if I lost a few pounds, I would be *gorgeous*.

Now, finally, I felt fulfilled. I had stopped eating junk food, like french fries and chocolates. When I was hungry, I snapped my fingers until the urge to eat passed. For the first time, I was the owner of myself. At such a young age, I had the guts the other girls didn't. It wasn't my fault that they wanted to be a bunch of fat losers. Successful girls work day and night. We are perfect, and we look perfect.

That same weekend I had a big project to finish for my science class. But I'd do it later. At the time, the most important thing was to be at my birthday party, although the only thing that really excited me was to wear my new violet dress.

I put it on, but I felt I was freezing within two minutes of wearing it. But, of course, the dress had short sleeves! Who wouldn't feel that way?

"Mom, can you turn on the heat, please? It feels like the North Pole!"

"No wonder you walk like a penguin, ha, ha, ha," said Rodrigo, my 15-year-old brother.

"Rodrigo, don't be mean to your sister! I will turn on the heat, even though the bill is expensive and it's really not cold at all. But hey, who's the birthday girl? Reb, are you sure you're not going to have breakfast? You haven't had a bite since yesterday morning!"

"Mom, I already told you that I will eat at the party, once everyone's here."

But I wasn't planning on eating when everyone was there. Instead, all weekend I was fasting to lose some weight and get in shape in time for my next competition.

"Mom, this is a branch of hell. Turn off the heat!" Rodrigo complained.

"Mom, where's Dad?" I asked.

"He had an emergency at work. But he promised to be here for your party."

"Whatever, I don't care," I replied as my heart shrank.

People began to arrive.

I saw Esther approaching me with a slime kit and a box of chocolates. The first gift made me outraged because I was no longer a girl from first grade who played with slime, but the second one unleashed a rage that was impossible to contain. That box of chocolates probably had over one thousand calories. I had become an expert at calculating the calories in food and how long it would take to burn them with exercise.

"Are you crazy? What were you thinking?" - I yelled at Esther without any empathy.

My friend and her mom stared at me, puzzled. Rodrigo went to look for my mom to bring her to the scene.

"What do you mean, Reb?" Esther said.

"How can you bring me a box of chocolates as a gift?" Don't you know I'm training for my next competition? These are gonna make me as fat and slow as you! You want me to lose, right? You want me to be ugly and unsuccessful again. Of course, all of you are dying of envy because you are not like me!" I exploded.

"Rebecca!" It was my mom's firm voice behind me.

"What nonsense are you saying?! Apologize to your friend right now!"

I went crazy. Tears slid down my cheeks uncontrollably and, after giving a desperate cry, I ran upstairs to my room. Halfway up the stairs, I stumbled and heard the girls' laughter. I went on and slammed the door.

I didn't go down to the living room again that afternoon. I heard the music continue. After insisting twice, my mother gave up: no human force managed to detach me from the mattress where I was crying face down. I would miss my own birthday party. I found out later that my mom apologized to my friend and her family while I was in my room.

My dad didn't find out about it until late that night, when he came home, exhausted and bitter. I felt precisely the same.

"I'm sorry, Honey! I tried to get out as soon as possible but I couldn't," my dad explained to my mom.

"While you deal with your reports, I have to deal with your daughter all by myself. She's got me worried," mom replied.

"Rebecca? How come? She's an excellent student and does wonderfully at skating. What happened?"

"It so happened that your skating princess threw a huge tantrum during her own birthday party, which, by the way, she missed, just like you."

"What do you mean she missed her party? What happened?"

I was listening to everything at the top of the stairs. Mom told dad, in great detail, what had happened.

"I think we should get her out of figure skating, at least for a while," my mother said as my little heart began to break into pieces like smashed sand.

I appeared as fast as a bolt of lightning in front of my parents and asked them to punish me, to leave me without television, to do whatever they wanted, but to please don't take me out of figure skating.

My mom, visibly upset and worried, told me that she would think about it but that I'd have to eat dinner first because I hadn't eaten the entire day. I replied that that was the only thing I couldn't do to please her. If I got fat, my new suits wouldn't fit me. I cried and got down on my knees. Then, holding on to her right leg, I begged her to please not force me to eat or leave my skating competitions.

"My love, I am not forcing you. You have to eat, you have to if you want to continue in competitions. I already told you that you're as skinny as those pink shoelaces you love."

"That's true, princess," my dad said.

"You're all against me!" I retorted hysterically while drowning in my own tears. "You all want to see me fat again!"

"But you've never been fat, my love," Dad said.

"Yes, I was fat, and nobody loved me back then. I couldn't jump in the air or have cute outfits. And you want me to be like that again!"

"What are you saying?" intervened mom.

My brother Rodrigo listened to the entire conversation from the living room. Instead of mocking me, he remained silent and, for the first time in a long time, he had nothing clever to express.

The week after that altercation, my parents took me to a therapist. Unfortunately, neither the tantrums nor the begging I imposed on them for a few days prevented it. My only consolation was that my skating workouts hadn't been canceled.

Claudia, my therapist, showed me videos of several girls — and boys, too — who had suffered from something called *Anorexia Nervosa.* I discovered that I was not the only one who felt this way. There were more people with symptoms and thoughts that were remarkably similar to mine. We all had an excessive fear of eating and gaining weight, of *looking ugly*, a fear of people stopping loving and flattering us.

"Lanugo" turned out to be the name of the tiny hairs that appeared on my body.

Claudia also told me that the sadness, irritability, and cognitive rigidity — that is to say, I was stubborn — were consequences of the poor diet I was feeding my brain with.

"But we eat for our body, not for our brain," I interjected.

"And our brain is not part of our body? Is it not an organ that exists, gets sick, and heals just like our heart or our stomach?"

I had never seen it that way.

"We don't usually think about it much until we need it. But not to worry, you're going to be fine, Rebecca. Of course, we'll need the help of a nutritionist to give you a healthy diet based on your lifestyle. And we will need to work together in therapy for a while. You know that your parents brought you here because they love you with all their hearts and want to help you, right?"

Unable to avoid it, I burst into tears.

Thanks to Claudia, I learned that year after year, there are thousands of cases of people, mainly girls, who die from this disorder. It can cause a person to sink into a well from which it is difficult to get out.

She told me about laxatives, vomiting, and black and white ideas, such as "Lettuce is good; chocolate is bad." She told me that girls like me go into more advanced stages and begin to physically harm themselves. Some start to pinch their skin. Some do way more serious things.

After several therapy sessions, some of them with my family, I understood that my parents were not my enemies. My physical appearance had become an obsession, and they only wanted to prevent that from escalating. They did not want me to end up like the kids that Claudia showed me, many of whom died of cardiac arrest and malnutrition.

Despite all this knowledge, it wasn't easy to overcome the fear of gaining weight once the treatment had started. I felt a pang of inexplicable guilt inside me. I didn't want to look in the mirror or take pictures of myself. But facing my ghosts was a worthwhile fight.

Little by little, I began to understand that I did deserve to eat, that I did deserve to live. I understood that I didn't have to *earn* the calories I consumed.

My family also understood that the solution was way more complex than simply saying to me, "You've got to eat more." Little by little, I recognized and positively used the emotions I was experiencing, such as fear, sadness, anger, and guilt.

I silenced that inner voice that told me that what I was doing wasn't enough. That I was not enough, that I could always be prettier, win more skating competitions, and be more likable to other children and adults. I kept hearing this voice, but I knew it was wrong.

The whole process was complicated. There were times when I wanted to give up; I felt like going back to the situation I was in before because it was more comfortable. But Claudia, my nutritionist, and my family — yes, even Rodrigo — didn't leave me alone. They held onto me tightly before I completely fell into a well from which it would've been even more challenging to get out.

Today, four years after that episode, I am excited to think about what I will eat after my skating practice. I enjoy food and know it is my friend and source of life, not my enemy.

I know that I will always have to work with a lot of patience, confidence, and self-esteem, to keep this balance and my healthy behaviors. Still, the effort is worth it. It is worth all the – real – happiness in the world.

No more loneliness, anxiety, or death. Just ice rinks, family dinners, and lots of new friends who value me for who I am, not for what I weigh or how I look.

Now I am the one who hugs those shoelaces before skating, not the one who hugs like a lace. Now, I hug with a heart full of joy, and a belly full of delicious, nutritious food.

See you in the next live! Love!

CPSIA information can be obtained
at www.ICGtesting.com
Printed in the USA
LVHW070114150322
713474LV00008B/130